Why Do Bullies Bully?

Written and Illustrated By:
Rachel Godfrey

Hello, my name is Rachel. Not only do I stutter and have a learning disability, I also have two lazy eyes. Kids called me, "Crazy Eyes"!

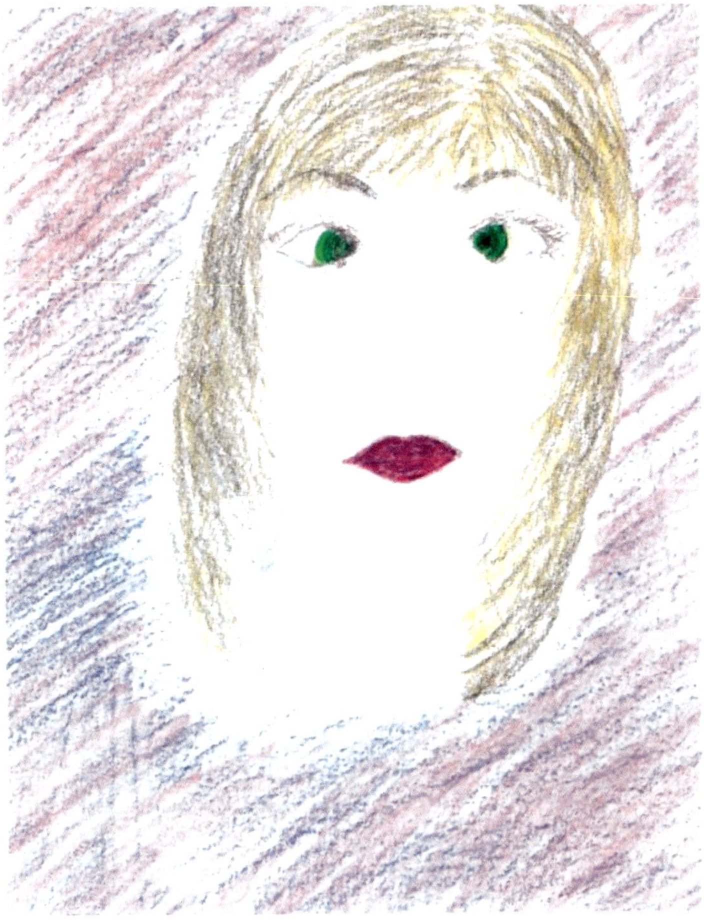

Whenever I stuttered, bullies would start talking like I did and laugh, just like they did in elementary school.

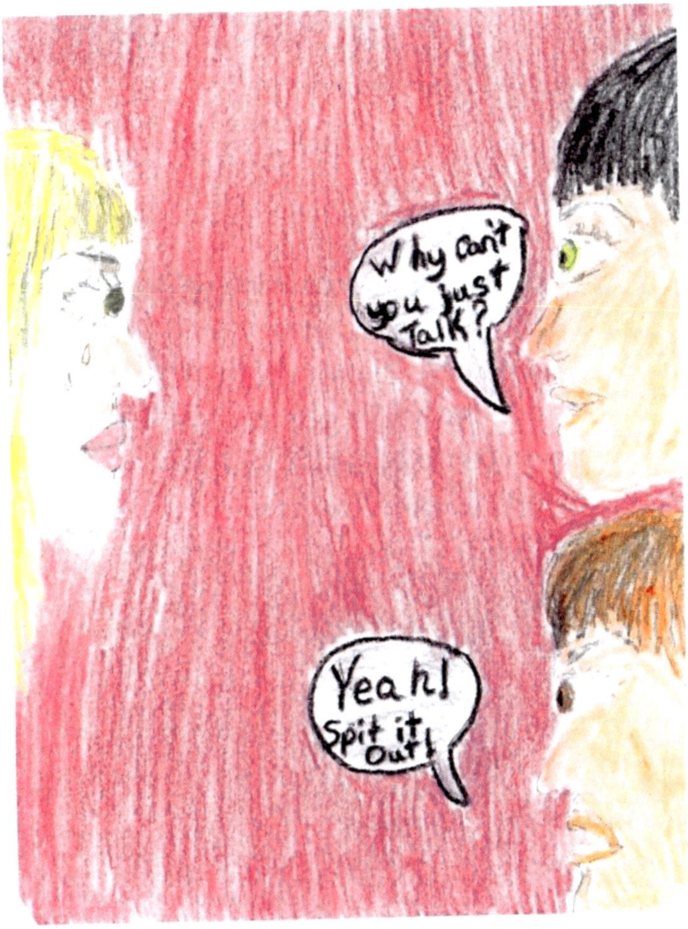
Why can't you just Talk?
Yeah! Spit it out!

I also had to go to a classroom where students learned at a slower pace. Bullies wouldn't care if they were late getting to their own classes. They would wait for me to get to mine and laugh at me.

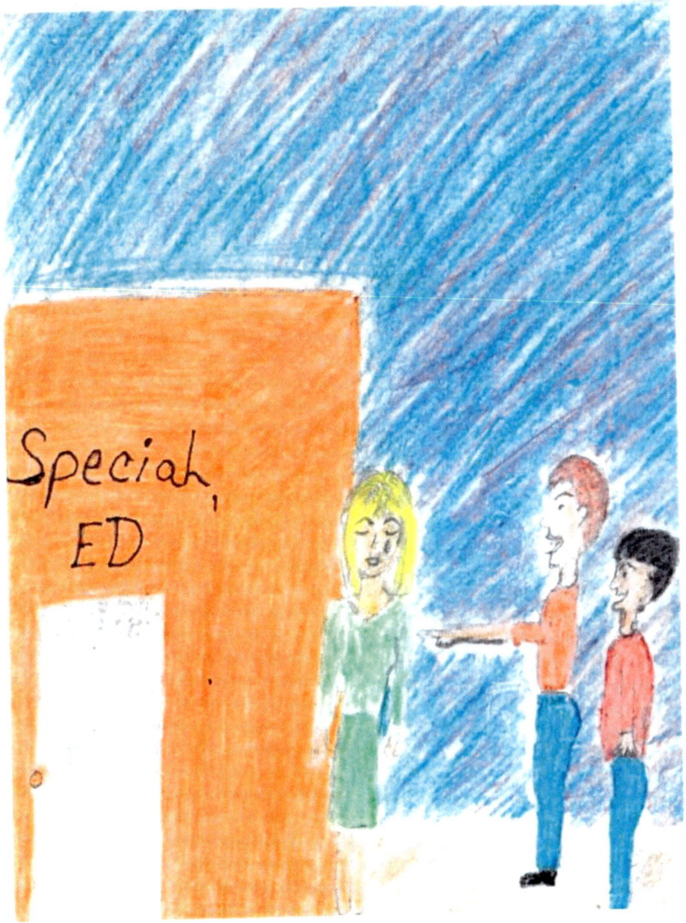
Special
ED

Bullies found me in the restroom, my classroom, my locker and of all buses, they rode mine.

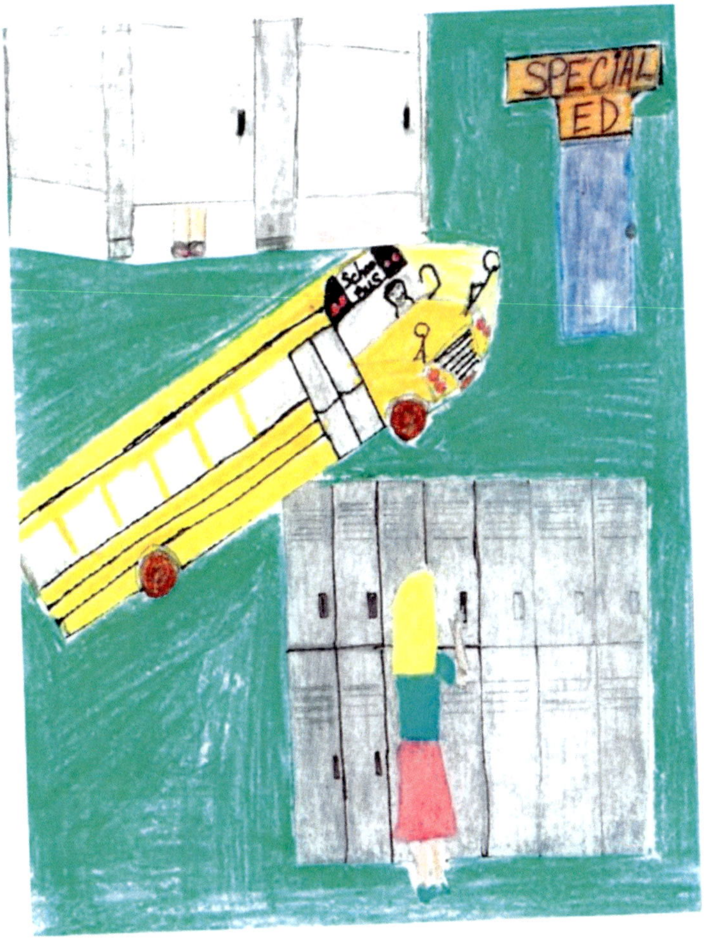

SPECIAL
ED

I hated riding the bus. Spitballs were thrown at my head and when I got up for my bus stop, they tripped me.

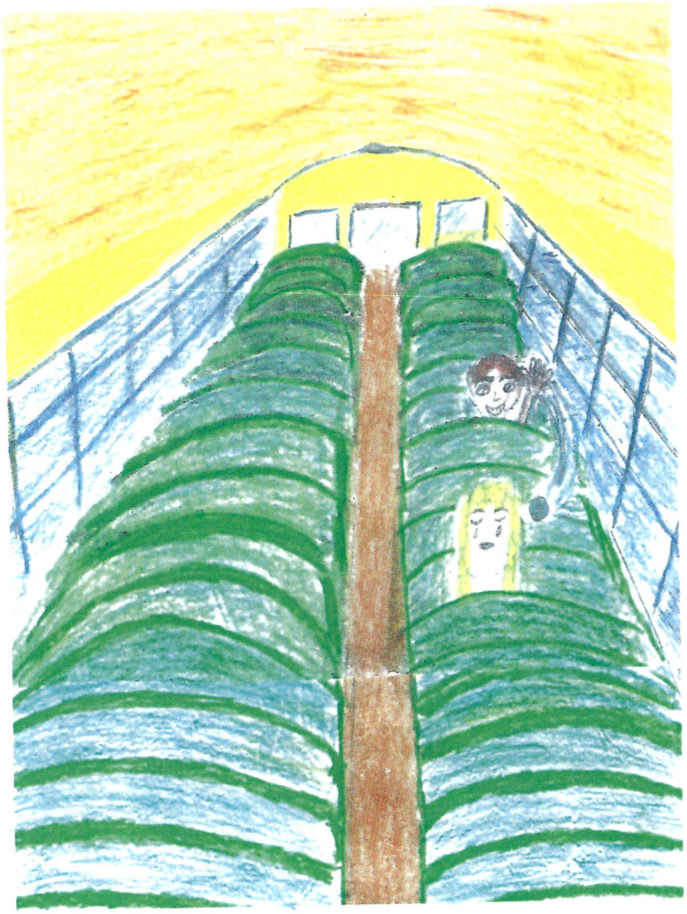

No matter where I hid, they always found me. It was like they had radar and antennas on their heads.

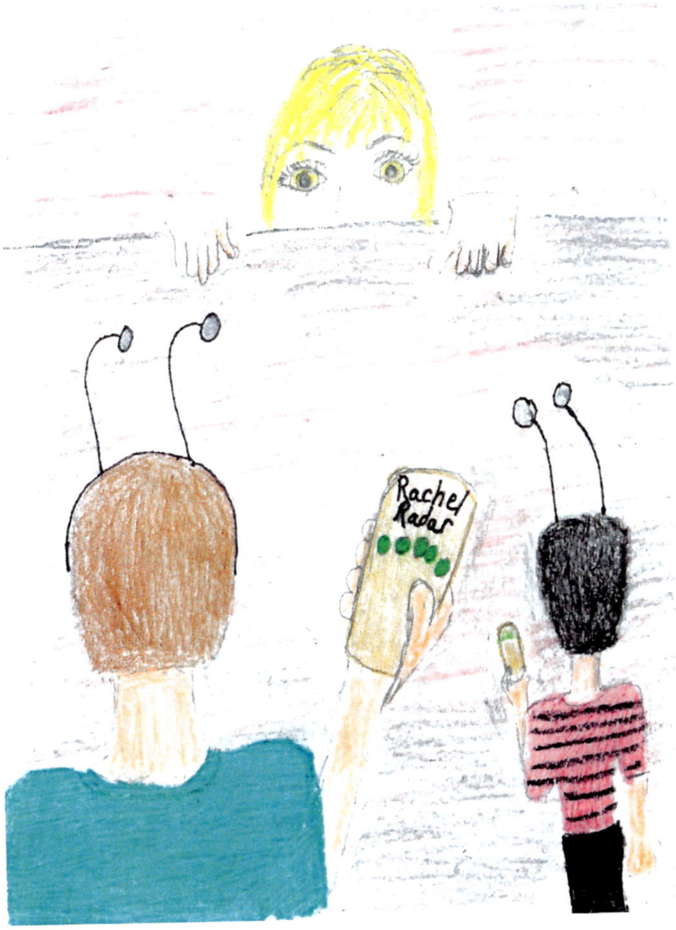
Rachel Radar

Bullies would quietly bother me so the teacher wouldn't notice them. I would get really mad and yell out, "Leave me alone!" The teacher gave me detention for disturbing the class. What's up with that?

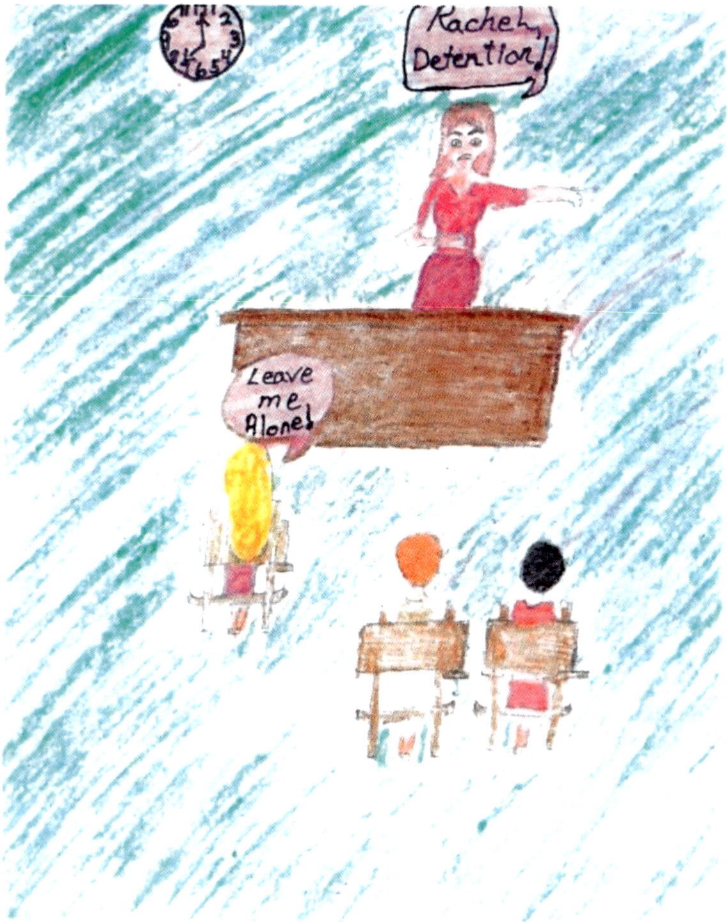
Rachel, Detention!
Leave me Alone!

I would be at my locker and as I reached for my books, they would slam the locker-door on my hand. "OUCH!"

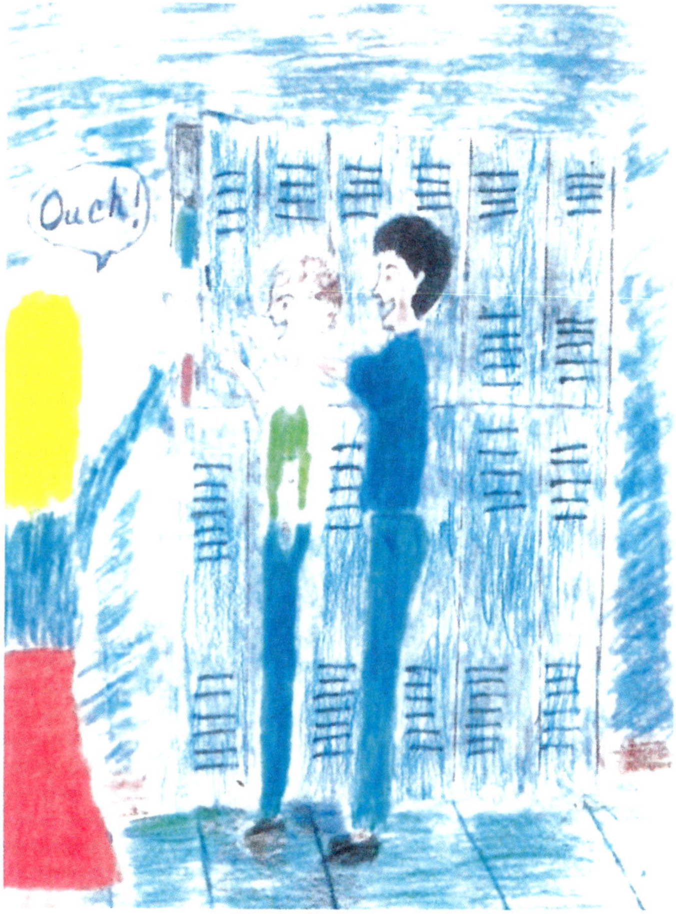
Ouch!

I noticed that bullies almost always had others backing them up. Wow, imagine that! My bully was a coward.

Whenever anybody said anything mean to me, I would reply, "Sorry you feel that way," because it was their loss. They judged me without getting to know me.

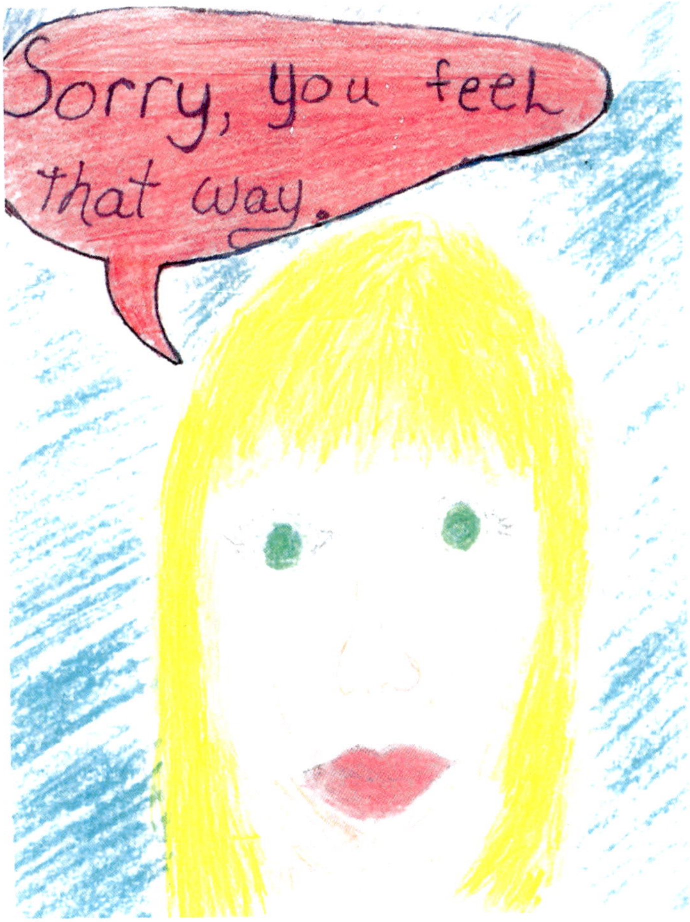
Sorry, you feel that way.

Please understand that it is something the bully doesn't like about him or herself so they put others down to make themselves feel better.

Just in case the bully doesn't stop, I still tell a grown-up because they no longer say, "Just ignore it." They now set consequences to put an end to bullying.

About The Author

I came into this world on April 26, 1971, with only one-third of my thyroid gland. This lead to other deficits which included a learning disability, speech and hearing impairments, slow motor skills and delayed reflexes. I also had two lazy eyes which were later corrected. I don't recall a time when I wasn't being bullied. Unfortunately, bullies don't always grow out of this behavior, but it's nice to know that there is a way we can deal with them without feeling defeated.